D0518217

Renaissance People

Sarah Howarth

The Millbrook Press
Brookfield, Connecticut

For Patrick and Catherine

Published in the United States in 1992 by
The Millbrook Press
2 Old New Milford Road
Brookfield Connecticut 06804

First published in Great Britain in 1992 by
Simon & Schuster Young Books
Campus 400
Maylands Avenue
Hemel Hempstead
Hertfordshire HP2 7EZ

Designed by Neil Adams
Illustrations by Philip McNeill

Text copyright © 1992 by Sarah Howarth
Illustrations copyright © 1992 by Philip McNeill

Typeset by DP Press Ltd, Sevenoaks

Printed and bound by Proost International Book Co., Belgium

Library of Congress Cataloging-in-Publication Data

Howarth, Sarah.
  Renaissance people/Sarah Howarth.
    p.   cm.
  Includes bibliographical references and index.
  Summary: Presents thirteen walks of life from the Renaissance,
including banker, artist, and explorer. Includes quotations from
contemporary sources.
    ISBN 1–56294–088–0
    1. Manners and customs—History—Juvenile literature.
2. Renaissance—Juvenile literature.   3. Europe—Social life and
customs—Juvenile literature.   [1. Renaissance.]   I. Title.
GT130.H68 1992
391'.0094'09024–dc20   92–4990
                                                                   CIP
                                                                    AC

Picture acknowledgments

Picture research by Caroline Mitchell

Front cover: Scala
Spine: Bridgeman Art Library

Ancient Art & Architecture Collection: p.10, p.12, p.17, p.23, p.28, p.29, p.35; Archivi
Alinari: p.7; Bildarchiv Preussischer Kulturbesitz: p.41; Bridgeman Art Library: p.11
(Vatican Museum), p.18, p.27, p.42 (Prado, Madrid), p.43, p.44; British Museum: p.9; The
Burrell Collection, Glasgow Museums: p.19; ET Archive: p.39; Mary Evans Picture Library:
p.32, p.33, p.36; Giraudon: p.30; Herzog Anton Ulrich Museum: p.8; Michael Holford: p.15;
Kunshistorisches Museum, Vienna: p.31; Mansell Collection: p.13, p.20, p.24, p.40, p.45;
Musee Cantonal, Lausanne: p.34; Ann Ronan Picture Library: p.37; By kind permission of
the Marquess of Tavistock and the Trustees of the Bedford Estates: p.14; Scala: p.22;
Syndication International/British Tourist Authority: p.16; Walters Art Gallery: p.25;
Wellcome Institute Library, London: p.38; Victoria and Albert Museum: p.21; ZEFA: p.26

CONTENTS

INTRODUCTION

Imagine you had to tell someone from another planet about life in the twentieth century. How would you do it? One way to start would be to give the period a title that would sum up its most important events.

This book will tell you about life in the fifteenth and sixteenth centuries, a period of European history known as the Renaissance. This word comes from the French language and means ''rebirth'' or ''reawakening.'' Many historians use this title because it sums up what they believe to have been the most significant development of the time: a rebirth of interest in the classical world of ancient Greece and Rome.

This revival of interest led to many changes. It particularly affected how people looked at the world, and their beliefs about what the human race could do. Many new and exciting ideas developed. There were new ways of making money; new ways of thinking about power, politics, and war; new ideas about science and religion; new designs for building; new ways to write and paint. Meanwhile, voyages of exploration brought Europeans to distant countries that were new to them. It was a time of great optimism.

You can find out about these developments, and how they began to change society, by looking at the life and work of the different Renaissance people described in this book.

THE BANKER

Here an Italian bookseller who lived in the fifteenth century tells us how a wealthy merchant and banker named Cosimo de' Medici arranged to pay wages to a sculptor working for him:

He told the bank to pay money each week to Donatello for his work and that of his four assistants.

The first banks

The first banks were very different from banks today. The word "bank" comes from a Latin word that simply means "bench" or "table." The bench was the sort of little stall that might be found in the market square of an important city. On this bench, the "banker" set out his notebooks, a pile of coins, and a set of scales to weigh them out. He was ready to do business.

Banking skills developed in the thriving towns of Italy in the Middle Ages and gradually spread to other countries. By the time of the Renaissance, there were many banks in Italy. Most were run by powerful family companies like the Medici and the Strozzi, but some were run by city authorities. Germany was another country famous for its banks, particularly those run by the Welser and Fugger families. These banks had changed a great deal since the days of the market stall. They operated from grand buildings and dealt in huge sums of money.

Bankers and wealthy merchants spent large sums of money on works of art. This picture was painted for a banker named Portinari, who worked in Bruges in the fifteenth century. It shows his wife and daughter kneeling in prayer at the feet of two saints.

The work of the banker

There were many different sorts of bankers. Some acted as pawnbrokers, and others as money changers, exchanging foreign coins into the money used locally for visiting pilgrims or merchants from different countries. Some lent people money, charging them interest on it (for example, they might lend $10 and expect to get $12 back). Some took money from their customers, agreeing to give it back at the end of a certain period of time, with interest added to the original sum.

Others helped people to make payments without money actually changing hands. To do this, they made a note in their books to show that money from one person's account should be added to another's account.

Many bankers were also merchants involved in long-distance trade, buying goods in one country and selling them elsewhere. They needed money on their travels, but because of the possibility of a surprise attack by robbers, it was dangerous to carry the gold and silver coins they required. So banking companies began to set up their own offices in other countries. They also provided documents called bills of exchange, which allowed a merchant from one country to obtain money from a bank in another. His own bank would take the money from his account and use it to repay the foreign bank for the money he had obtained.

All these developments meant that merchants did not have to carry great numbers of coins with them in order to do business.

Here you can see a banker at work in his office. Behind the two men are drawers labeled with the names of the countries with which the bank did business. How many can you count?

Making money make money

Some people were very suspicious of the work performed by bankers. *"All banks are thieves,"* said Michelangelo, one of the most admired artists of the Renaissance. He was expressing an opinion that most people shared. For many years the Church had taught that it was wrong to lend someone money in order to profit by making the borrower pay interest. This was called "usury" and was considered sinful. Because of these ideas, bankers and money-lenders were often very unpopular.

During the Renaissance, attitudes gradually began to change. The sixteenth-century French Protestant John Calvin was the first Church thinker to suggest that it was

not a sin to lend money and charge interest. He argued that borrowing and lending put money to good use. It could be invested in trade and so earn more money.

It was a long time before Calvin's view was widely accepted. Bankers still faced criticism. Despite this, more and more people came to them to lend or borrow —whether it was a sin or not! Even kings borrowed large sums to pay for their wars.

The money lent by banks was used to pay for art and building, trade and wars. You will find out more about these things in the following chapters.

Kings and queens needed money to pay for their wars. They wanted it to pay their soldiers, or to build and equip ships like this one. To do so, they often had to borrow money from the bankers.

THE ARTIST

A writer who lived in the sixteenth century describes how a famous Italian artist called Giotto was summoned by the king of Naples to paint pictures for him:

The king wanted Giotto to come to Naples at all costs, to decorate some new buildings for him. Giotto did a lot of work there. The king liked watching him work.

The artist's studio

The artist had to be a businessman as well as a painter: he had to sell his work to earn money. He worked according to the work people ordered from him, as other craftsmen did, and a popular artist might have many different commissions (orders) at any one time.

The artist's studio was a busy place. Young men and boys were taken on as apprentices, learning how to paint in return for help with all sorts of tasks. They fetched water, mixed the paint and varnish, and helped with the painting when they were good enough. There was sometimes fierce competition between different studios.

Princes and painters

In the Middle Ages, artists were not considered very important people. They rarely signed their names to their work, which is one reason why we know very little about them as individuals. In the Renaissance these things changed. Some artists won great fame and wealth. One contemporary said that the Italian artist Raphael lived *"more like a prince than a painter."* The story of Giotto and the king of Naples shows how the most popular artists might mix with nobility and royalty. These men were celebrities, not at all like the humble and anonymous craftsmen who came before them.

In this picture, an artist paints at an easel while his assistant is busy in the background. Artists were trained like other craftsmen. They learned as apprentices when they were young.

New ways to represent the world

Ever since the people of western Europe had been converted to Christianity, most paintings showed saints and stories from the Bible and were designed to be aids to prayer. They were not meant to record things in a life-like way.

Giotto, who lived in Italy at the end of the thirteenth century, painted in a different way. He wanted his pictures to look realistic. To do this, he used techniques that had not been practiced since the days of the ancient Greeks and Romans.

In the fifteenth and sixteenth centuries, artists all

over Europe became interested in this way of representing the world. They too wanted to draw things to make them look just as they appeared in real life. These people thought that medieval art seemed poor and old-fashioned. The art of ancient Greece and Rome became popular instead, and the most fashionable artists modeled their work on it. This was part of the new interest in classical culture that has led historians to name this period of history the Renaissance (rebirth) of classical ideas.

Two things made the new style of art stand out. The first was the very precise and scientific way in which the painters approached their subjects. They worked very

Here you can see one of the pictures Michelangelo painted for the Pope on the ceiling of the Sistine Chapel in Rome. It illustrates a scene from the Old Testament of the Bible, and shows God creating Adam.

hard to make objects in their paintings seem solid and to make the distance between them seem right. Artists also studied mathematics and geometry, eager to find new ways of representing what they saw in nature.

The second important change was a great pride in

This study of the human body was drawn by the famous Italian artist Leonardo da Vinci. Like Leonardo, many artists at this time aimed to draw and paint in a lifelike way. Artists had not done this since the days of ancient Greece and Rome.

human achievements. Renaissance artists took pleasure in recording every aspect of human life, from feasts and dancing to ordinary street scenes and fighting. They also painted landscapes and portraits. A good example is the work of the German artist Holbein, who painted many portraits of people in the court of Henry VIII of England.

A picture of the past

Because Renaissance artists painted such a wide range of subjects, we have a record of people, places, and events at this time that did not exist in the Middle Ages. Their art shows us what Renaissance people looked like—kings, queens, great scholars, even the artists themselves.

THE EXPLORER

Ｔhese are the plans made by an Italian explorer named Sebastian Cabot for an expedition from England to the East in the sixteenth century:

Winds permitting, the fleet will keep together. The captain, pilot-major, masters, and masters' mates will set the course. Every day a record will be made of how the ships are navigated.

Sailing to unknown countries

Travel was dangerous in the Middle Ages. Few ships could manage long journeys without being broken to bits by rough seas. Because of this, there were parts of the world about which the people of Europe knew nothing at all. It took a lot of courage to put to sea in a small boat, with a chart that might turn out to be wrong, and sail into the unknown. In the fifteenth and sixteenth centuries, explorers from different European countries did just that.

Making journeys for the first time

In these years Europeans reached many parts of the globe for the first time. From England, John and Sebastian Cabot sailed to Newfoundland in eastern Canada. Dutch explorers sailed north, becoming the first Europeans to land in Spitzbergen in the Arctic Ocean. Ferdinand Magellan of Portugal sailed around the tip of South America and into the Pacific. His expedition was the first to sail right around the world, although Magellan himself died on the journey.

Earning money by trade

Many voyages were undertaken to find new opportunities for trade. One sixteenth-century historian

Sailors had very simple equipment to help them navigate their ships. They plotted their course by looking at the position of the stars. This picture shows an explorer finding his position by looking at the stars.

tells us how the Portuguese, "*wanting to earn money by, trade, began to sail along the coast of Africa.*" They were hoping to find a sea route to the Spice Islands (now the Moluccas in Indonesia) in the Pacific.

The spice trade was very important at this time. Merchants grew rich by dealing in the spices that were in demand for cooking, such as pepper, cloves, nutmeg, and ginger. But before sailors found a sea route, the merchants of Europe could not safely buy supplies directly from the Islands. Instead they usually had to rely on rival merchants from other countries bringing these goods overland to markets they could reach. The European merchants knew they could make more money if they could travel safely to the islands themselves.

Here a sixteenth century artist has shown Queen Elizabeth I of England. Her hand rests on a globe, and there is a fleet of ships in the background. Elizabeth was very interested in the voyages made by explorers. So, too, were many other rulers.

Looking for a sea route to the Spice Islands

Expeditions sailed from many countries in the search for a sea route to the Spice Islands. Explorers had different ideas about how to get there. Some sailed west from Europe, believing that if the world was round they would eventually get to the East if they sailed far enough in this direction. Others sailed northwest or northeast.

A historian of the time tells the story of one expedition, led by an Italian sailor named Christopher Columbus in 1492. Columbus set sail from the Canary Islands and decided to head to the West:

Columbus obtained ships from the king and queen of Spain. After thirty-three days' sailing, he discovered some islands at the extreme end of our hemisphere. No one knew about these islands before.

Columbus believed he had almost reached his goal, the Spice Islands of the East, but he had in fact landed in the Bahamas. Others followed his route and realized that this was a land that Europeans had not known about before. This was the beginning of the European settlement of North and South America.

In the fifteenth and sixteenth centuries Europeans sailed to parts of the world (such as America) about which they knew nothing. Maps like this were drawn to show lands that were new to them.

While Columbus tried this way to the East, Portuguese explorers tried another. They hoped to sail around the southern tip of Africa and then go east, but Africa's coastline was longer than they had expected. Many sailors turned back without reaching the most southerly point, but each voyage brought new knowledge and at last success came. In 1488 an expedition led by Bartholomeu Dias rounded the Cape of Good Hope. Nine years later Vasco da Gama followed a similar route and sailed as far as India. The new sea route had been found at last.

Sailing ships

A ship was navigated by its captain, who found the way by looking at the position of the sun and stars. He might also use charts, a compass, and an instrument called an astrolabe.

A new type of ship that was designed at this time was called a caravel. The caravel had two or three masts and square sails. It could cope with stormy seas better than earlier ships and it was used on many voyages of exploration.

THE PRINCE

The busy routine of a fifteenth-century ruler is described by a contemporary in this way:

When the prince had already retired for the night, ready to go to bed, his secretary came with a pile of letters for him to read through and sign before he could sleep.

Different kinds of government

During the Renaissance there were many different kinds of governments. Most places were ruled by important noblemen and women. Some, like Spain and England, were kingdoms ruled by kings and queens. In others, such as Italy and Germany, independent nobles ruled over small states of their own. People at the time often used the word ''prince'' to describe the ruler— whether the ruler was a king, queen, duke, count, or emperor! In this book we will follow their example and use the word in this way, too.

This castle was built on the instructions of King Henry VIII of England. He feared that other European countries might attack his kingdom. The people expected their ruler to defend the country.

Power and fear

The power of many rulers became stronger during this period. In England, France, Spain, and the Netherlands, uprisings (rebellions) by powerful nobles had been squelched, leaving the prince stronger than ever before. But princes were always frightened that a rebellion might break out. Knowing that their power might be threatened, they were ruthless in dealing with any opposition. The story of Queen Elizabeth I of England and her rival, Mary, Queen of Scots, gives an example of this.

Elizabeth knew that there were plots to put Mary on the English throne, for both religious and political reasons. A contemporary said that Elizabeth *"feared not only for her throne, but also for her life."* When Mary came to England in 1568, Elizabeth had her imprisoned. Three different rebellions did break out, and the rebels hoped to make Mary queen of England. Finally Elizabeth gave the order for Mary's execution. It was too dangerous for Elizabeth to allow her cousin to live.

Of course, princes had always made hard decisions like this. But they found it difficult to justify such actions. Much had been written in the Middle Ages about how princes should behave. They were expected to lead good Christian lives. When medieval writers described the ideal ruler, they did not mention the sort of practical problems princes really faced, or the sort of decision Queen Elizabeth had to make.

Machiavelli's ideas about power

In 1513 an Italian called Niccolò Machiavelli wrote a book called *The Prince*, which described a new way of thinking about power. Unlike earlier writers, he pointed

Many princes displayed their wealth and power by living in grand style and paying for paintings and sculptures to show off in their homes. This statue by the sculptor Michelangelo, was ordered by the powerful Medici family in Florence in Italy.

out that princes must sometimes make unpleasant decisions.

Machiavelli explained that it was his aim *"to describe things as they really are, not how they are in the imagination."* He said that it was better for a prince to be feared than loved by his people, and that there were times when a prince would have to be cruel.

These ideas shocked people. Many thought Machiavelli's words were so evil that he must be working with the devil. But despite this, his book led to great changes in how people thought and wrote about politics in the future.

During the Renaissance, artists painted portraits for the first time. Because of this, we know what many princes and important people looked like. Here is a sixteenth century painting of Lorenzo the Magnificent, who ruled Florence from 1469–1492.

Signing piles of letters at night

The quotation at the beginning of this chapter shows how princes increased their control by keeping an eye on every detail of government. Kings like Philip II of Spain and Henry VIII of England set up councils to deal with important matters. The men that they picked as ministers and councillors were men who owed everything to the king. These were not necessarily the great aristocrats, but a new professional class of royal servants.

THE COURTIER

L ife at a duke's court in the sixteenth century is recorded for us by an Italian named Castiglione. He tells us that courtiers passed their time in:

jousting, tournaments, riding, and handling weapons, with masques and feasting, games, music, and all the activities suitable to noblemen.

The court: a center of power

The wealth and power of the prince made the court an important place. Political decisions and appointments to high positions in the prince's councils were made there.

Hunting was a very popular pastime for kings and queens and their courtiers. Here you can see courtiers hunting deer.

Men and women who were the prince's friends or trusted advisers received rich gifts as a mark of favor. These were the rewards of life at court. Only by being at court, living the life of a courtier, could the nobility hope to win these prizes.

A new way of life for the nobility

In the Middle Ages war dominated the nobles' way of life. In the Renaissance this began to change. The

Courtiers like those shown here, were expected to be able to sing and play music. They had to have many skills in order to take part in life at court.

nobleman was no longer simply a warrior; he became a courtier. The men and women who attended court were expected to have a wide range of accomplishments. The writer Castiglione describes these in his book, *The Courtier*. The men should be of noble birth, brave, skilled with weapons, well-mannered, educated, athletic, good at speaking and singing, and able to dance and play a variety of musical instruments. Even women now had a more important role in court life than they had in the Middle Ages.

The princes themselves were often skilled in all these fashionable accomplishments. Queen Elizabeth I of England spoke six languages, including Greek and Latin. She was a good dancer, composed poetry and was fond of music. A contemporary describes how another ruler, the duke of Urbino in Italy, not only had a passion for collecting books and works of art, but was also an excellent soldier.

As the life of the nobility became more civilized and less warlike, people wrote books giving rules and advice about how to behave. These included practical details about table manners—how to use a fashionable new instrument called the fork, for example. Castiglione's book was the most famous of all these books on manners.

Splendor with a political purpose

Many grand occasions were celebrated at court. Coronations, royal births and weddings, the signing of important treaties, or the visit of foreign princes were all accompanied by feasting and ceremony. Here an onlooker describes festivities held at court in Dresden in Germany when the prince's child was christened:

The tilting field was decorated magnificently. Tall fir trees were hung with pomegranates, oranges, and pumpkins. The prince marched with 100 huntsmen into the lists. They were all clad in green and made beautiful music. There was jousting that lasted for four days.

Princes all over Europe competed with each other to stage lavish and costly ceremonies like this at court. Such ceremony was not simply entertainment; there was also a political reason for it. The more extravagant the festivities, the more powerful and magnificent a prince was thought to be.

In 1520, Henry VIII of England and Francis I of France met each other at the "Field of the Cloth of Gold" in France to discuss a new treaty. The two kings were great rivals and their meetings were accompanied by elaborate ceremonies, which were designed to show how wealthy and powerful each king was. For two weeks the princes and their courtiers jousted, danced, and sang. Over six thousand workmen had been employed to build the pavilions where the courtiers spent their time. The events were so grand and impressed contemporaries so much, that they called this meeting the eighth wonder of the world.

This miniature shows the rich and elaborate costume worn by courtiers in the late sixteenth century. Many found that life at court was very expensive.

21

THE MERCENARY

The people of the fifteenth and sixteenth centuries believed that war was becoming more and more terrifying. They suggested several reasons for this. One was the use of mercenaries—professional soldiers who hired themselves out for pay. These men were widely feared. Machiavelli, the Italian writer and politician, wrote:

They are disunited, thirsty for power, undisciplined, and disloyal.

New ways of making war

Warfare was changing. In the Middle Ages, battles were fought by knights on horseback. For these men, war was a way of life. Although war was always violent and

Because of changes in the way war was fought, war was no longer the most important part of a nobleman's life. Many nobles, and even successful mercenaries, spent their time and energy on the building of splendid palaces and the creation of elaborate gardens. Here you can see a Renaissance palace and garden.

BELVEDER CON PITTI

bloody, it was supposed to be waged according to a set of rules known as the code of chivalry. A historian who lived at the time of the Renaissance noted how war was changing. *"We had been used to seeing wars staged with beautiful pomp and display, not unlike a spectacle,"* he explained, talking of the old days of knighthood. But now suddenly there were *"new fashions, new and bloody ways of making war."*

Mercenaries and gunpowder

The changes that most worried contemporaries were the gradual disappearance of the old ideals of chivalry, the new part played by mercenaries in battle, and the development of gunpowder.

This statue by the sculptor Verrocchio can still be seen in Venice, Italy. It was erected to honor a mercenary soldier. Many Italian city-states hired mercenaries to fight for them.

Many mercenaries fought in Italy, where they were involved in struggles between rival cities like Milan and Florence. In Italy these mercenaries were called *condottieri*. An Englishman named Sir John Hawkwood was a famous *condottiere*, who fought for many different Italian cities and princes. Some *condottieri* acquired great power for themselves, like Francesco Sforza, who became duke of Milan in 1450.

Mercenaries had a poor reputation. If their employers were slow in paying them, the mercenaries might riot. This happened in 1527, when parts of the city of Rome were destroyed by Emperor Charles V's mercenary force. The whole of Europe was horrified by the news.

Gunpowder was first used in Europe at this time. This made a great difference in the way war was fought. The first guns and cannons were often unreliable and not very accurate, but in time they changed warfare completely. No longer were the high walls of towns and castles a safe defense; now they could easily be overcome.

Going to war

Countries went to war for many reasons. Princes declared war in the hope of winning glory and riches by conquering other lands. As their power became

stronger at home, they wanted to go on foreign wars to add still more to their wealth and reputation. This is shown by the rivalry between three of the most powerful rulers; of the sixteenth century: Henry VIII of England; Francis I of France; and Charles V, the Holy Roman Emperor. Each dreamed of controlling the whole of Europe and spent vast amounts of money to further his ambition. When Henry VIII captured the fortress of Tournai in France, Francis I bought it back in 1518 for 600,000 crowns.

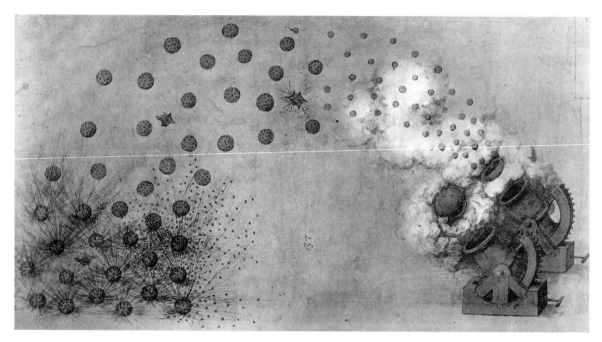

This drawing by Leonardo da Vinci shows his design for a cannon. Cannons were used for the first time in war in Europe in these years. When people first saw what they could do they were horrified.

Wars were also fought over religion. After the Protestant Reformation in the mid-sixteenth century, Christianity was divided and there was much bitterness between the different groups. Few rulers would tolerate their subjects adopting beliefs different from their own. In France this led to a time of civil war known as the "Wars of Religion," which lasted for many years. The differences between Catholics and Protestants also brought about war between the countries of Europe. Many princes went to war to defend their religion. The desire to uphold Catholicism was one of the reasons that Philip II of Spain sent a great invasion fleet called the Armada against Protestant England.

THE ARCHITECT

Architects were responsible for building design and construction. A passage written in the sixteenth century describes the sort of problem they had to solve in their work:

The architect had to design buildings for a monastery set in the slope of a mountain. He decided to make use of the foundation for cellars, bakehouses, stables, kitchens, and stores.

The work of the architect

Architects worked for a wide range of customers. They designed banks and town halls for merchants and members of guilds (trade organizations). Noblemen and women asked them for splendid palaces and great fortresses. Churchmen commissioned church and cathedral buildings from them. But these were not the only projects on which architects worked. They might also be called on for harbors, dams, bridges, libraries, and fortifications. The famous Italian artist Leonardo da Vinci (1452–1519) boasted that he could make portable bridges for use in war. Other Italian artists included Michelangelo, who worked on fortifications (defenses)

This picture tells us what Renaissance people thought towns should look like. The buildings are based on the classical designs of ancient Greece and Rome, which had become very popular. The designs are very regular, and architects studied mathematics to help create them.

for the city of Florence, and Brunelleschi, who designed dams for the prince of Mantua.

Because architecture was not looked on as a job in its own right at this time, men who worked as architects had many other skills. Da Vinci listed his accomplishments as painting, sculpture, architecture, and the manufacture of a variety of machines of war, including *"catapults, mangonels and other machines of marvelous efficacy not in common use."*

The ruins of ancient Rome

A contemporary tells a story about the famous architect Brunelleschi (1377–1446) that helps to explain a great change that was taking place in the way buildings were designed. He describes Brunelleschi's first journey to Rome as a young man, and the influence that the ruins of ancient buildings there made on him. *"He kept stopping in amazement,"* the account reveals.

The buildings of ancient Rome were planned and built in accordance with the rules of proportion. That means they were built according to very regular patterns, with the shape and size of each part balanced to fit in with the rest. During the Middle Ages, other architectural styles became fashionable and the Roman tradition of building fell out of use.

This photograph shows the city of Florence, Italy, and its cathedral. The great dome of the cathedral was designed by the architect, Brunelleschi. He studied the buildings of ancient Rome in order to draw up his plans.

But in Italy, which had been the center of the Roman Empire, and particularly in Rome, many classical buildings were still standing. Brunelleschi was just one of many visitors to Rome at this time. They were all excited by what they saw. Architects like Brunelleschi studied the ruins carefully, measuring them and examining the way they had been built. Soon architects were making attempts to design new buildings in the classical style. First in Italy, and then all over Europe, architects began to base their work on Roman examples. This was yet another way in which classical civilization influenced the art of the fifteenth and sixteenth centuries. The result can still be seen today in many Italian cities.

The architects of this period who looked to ancient Rome for inspiration and ideas set a trend that has continued right up to the twentieth century. If you look carefully at great houses and public buildings designed after the Renaissance, such as Monticello in Charlottesville, Virginia, you will see that they too have been influenced by the style of the ancient Romans and by the masters of the Renaissance.

Here you can see the Italian city of Florence as it looked to a fifteenth-century painter. If you look closely, you can see the city walls and defenses, bridges, the cathedral, and fine houses. Renaissance architects worked on all sorts of building projects like these.

Buildings and books

By 1485 a book had been printed to help architects who were eager to follow the new ideas. It was the work of an Italian called Alberti, who was an architect, poet, mathematician, art critic, engineer, and writer on a wide range of subjects. His book helped to spread the newly rediscovered knowledge of Roman architecture.

The new structures also helped to introduce people to the building techniques of ancient Rome. In Florence in Italy, work had begun on a new cathedral in 1296. More than one hundred years later it had not been finished, because the nave and aisles (central area) were very wide, and the architects could not decide how to construct a roof to fit over this enormous space. It was Brunelleschi who solved the problem, thanks to his painstaking study of Roman buildings.

THE WRITER

The great Italian scientist, Galileo Galilei (1564–1642), wrote that:

I should like my books to become one of my main sources of income . . . There are many I want to work on: two on the universe, three on movement, three on mechanics, others on sound, color, the tides, the movement of animals, war—and many more.

An infinite range of knowledge

As you can see, Galileo had a wide range of interests. He worked as a teacher, mathematician, and astronomer. He was skilled in art and music, and he also found time to write books about his research. During this period, men and women who received an education wanted to be experts in as many different areas of knowledge as they could. Historians use the name "Renaissance man" to describe those who, like Galileo, were good at many different subjects. As one contemporary put it, they seemed to possess "*an infinite range of knowledge.*" Although this was an exaggeration, it certainly sums up the ideal of the time.

The use of the printing press in Europe in the middle of the fifteenth century meant that more people could buy books. Soon it was a common sight to see people selling books and newspapers in the streets, like the man in the picture.

Writers' careers

Because of this ideal, the men and women who wrote books in the fifteenth and sixteenth centuries were usually also involved in many other activities. If we look at some of the most famous books and authors of the time, you will see this very clearly. The career of the English author Thomas More (1478–1535) is a good example. In his book *Utopia*, More describes the imaginary island of Utopia and its inhabitants. He meant the work to criticize many aspects of English life and, by contrast, to show how society should be organized.

But, like Galileo, More was not only a writer. He was also a lawyer, a member of Parliament, one of Henry VIII's most important government officials, a scholar, and a theologian (expert on religious ideas). A member of More's family related how the king used to summon him so that they could talk together. Their conversations *"sometimes touched on astronomy, geometry or divinity, sometimes other sciences."*

More was not unusual. These are lines from a poem written by someone whose talents were just as varied:

all day my paintbrush
Spatters a rich mosaic upon my face.

Reading this, you might suspect that the author did not spend all his time writing, and you would be correct. The poem was written by Michelangelo, who was a painter, sculptor, architect, and poet.

Writing about anything and everything

In the Middle Ages, most books and poems had been inspired by religion. From the fifteenth century onward, this began to change. Books were written about ancient history, the history of more recent times, the lives of famous men and women, politics, literature, religion, science, art, war—the list seemed to be endless. The new invention of the printing press in the mid-fifteenth century helped this development.

We have already met some of the writers, such as Machiavelli, author of books on politics, history, and war (he also wrote plays), and Castiglione, author of the book about the ideal courtier. Then there was the bookseller from Florence, who decided to write about the famous men and women he had known, many of whom had come to his shop to buy books. And there were many others—like Queen Margaret of Navarre, who wrote a collection of stories, Vittoria Colonna, the poet, and the learned Dutch scholar Erasmus.

This picture was used in a book called Utopia *which was written by the Englishman, Thomas More. More worked as one of King Henry VIII's advisers and was a scholar as well as a writer. He was very interested in the classical world of ancient Greece and Rome.*

Here a writer presents a book to King Francis I of France. Many kings and queens were eager to encourage the work of writers and scholars.

People were curious about almost anything and everything human beings could do, or had done in the past, particularly in the days of ancient Greece and Rome. A new word was used to describe writers and scholars like More and Erasmus who were influenced by this ancient civilization. They were called "humanists."

THE CRAFTSMAN

The autobiography of a sixteenth-century Italian sculptor and goldsmith named Cellini tells us about the fine work done by Renaissance craftsmen:

I made a piece of silver in low relief, the size of a child's hand. It was to be worn as the buckle of a man's belt. On it I carved a bunch of leaves, cherubs, and beautiful masks. I made this in Francesco Salimbene's workshop. The members of the goldsmith's guild praised it highly.

The gold salt shaker shown here was made in the sixteenth century. We know a lot about it because the craftsman who made it wrote about his life and work. His name was Cellini. Cellini lived in Italy. He made the salt shaker for the king of France.

Working by hand

At this time all goods were made by hand by craftsmen and craftswomen. The records of many towns provide

us with information about these people and their work. Their names and occupations might be recorded when they had to pay tax, or because they were members of the guilds, which supervised the way business was done. Sources like these tell us that the inhabitants of fifteenth-century Florence, Italy, included silversmiths, cabinetmakers, tailors, sculptors, rope makers, weavers, wool carders, stocking makers, silk workers, and many cloth manufacturers.

The workshop

Today goods are produced in factories on a very large scale. In the Renaissance, goods were generally made on a small scale in workshops that were owned and run by a master craftsman. Helped by his family, perhaps one or two apprentices learning the trade, and a few employees, the craftsman not only made goods in the workshop—he sold them there as well. A man who lived in an Italian city at this time describes a working household of this sort:

This scene shows clockmakers in their workshop. Craftsmen sold their wares from their workshops. Here a customer has come to look at the clocks.

There was a man who worked as a weaver of velvet. He had many children and needed some help with his business, so he decided that he would make one of them learn to weave velvets too.

Craftsmen, such as painters, printers, sculptors, and jewelers, traded from their workshops in towns all over Europe.

The scale of business grows

As time went by, some businesses, such as cloth manufacturing, began to expand. Their owners employed workers and set up a number of workshops. Rather than working as craftsmen themselves, the owners spent their money on expanding the business.

Sometimes two or more people joined together to run their business as a partnership, so that they could trade on a larger scale and share the risks involved. Here the diary of a fifteenth-century merchant tells us about how an arrangement like this might work:

I began to work in the silk trade, and after ten years I became a partner. I had to invest 300 florins in the business . . . I did very well out of it all.

This kind of business organization was most common in Italy, but it spread to other European countries.

Merchandise fit for kings

The work of some craftsmen became more specialized. Instead of making objects for everyday use, they produced luxury goods that only the rich could afford. Cellini tells how he worked for years to make an elaborate gold saltcellar for the king of France:

When I brought it to the king, he gasped and could not take his eyes from it.

In this picture you can see the inside of a mill in which paper was made. Most goods were made by hand, but the papermakers used water power to help them in their work. You can see the wheels of the paper mill through the window.

Not all craftsmen worked for kings, but many earned a good reputation because of their skilled work. Italy had its goldsmiths who worked with precious metals and jewels. Germany was famed for metalworkers who made some of the finest armor of the time. Other German craftsmen led the way in new developments such as printing, clock and watchmaking, making guns, and the manufacture of precise instruments such as the astrolabe. In France, Protestant craftsmen became famous as makers of cloth, lace, hats, stockings, silk, and glass. In the Netherlands, craftsmen working with glass and lenses made the first microscopes and telescopes.

THE PROTESTANT

T his is how a historian who lived at the time described the beginnings of the Protestant faith:

New teachings against the Roman Church began to spread widely. This poisonous doctrine started in part of Germany called Saxony because of the preaching of a monk named Martin Luther.

Protestantism was a revolutionary movement in the Christian Church. Protestants broke away from the Catholic Church of Rome and organized religious life in their own way. These developments cause a great deal of argument.

Calling for change

Bitter disagreement over religious change broke out in many places. In France (shown here), there was civil war as Catholics and Protestants fought each other.

By the fifteenth century there were people in many European countries who felt unhappy about some parts of the teachings and traditions of the Catholic Church. Many different things worried them. Some people were not satisfied with the clergy. They believed that some Church leaders were corrupt—concerned only with power and wealth. The Italian poet Dante was just one of those who were critical of this state of affairs. He called the popes and high clergymen *"mouths of greed, gaping for gold and silver."*

A number of the popes of the fifteenth and sixteenth centuries earned a very bad reputation. Pope Alexander VI, at the end of the fifteenth century, was especially famous for the way he made his relations rich, particularly his favorite son, Cesare Borgia. A contemporary explains how Alexander and Cesare

hired assassins and used poison against their enemies. *"This was to take revenge and also because of their terrible greed,"* he writes. He tells us that people were losing respect for the Church and calling for change because of men like Alexander.

Relics to stop rain

There were other developments that led people to ask questions and criticize the Church. For centuries Christians had made pilgrimages to pray at the shrines of different saints. Devotion to relics (items believed to have belonged to a saint, or to have been a part of his or her body) had been an important part of popular religion. But now some people began to look at relics differently. Traditional beliefs were shaken when it was suggested that many were fakes. Here a Welsh writer lists a few of the relics in an English abbey:

the coals that burned St. Lawrence, the clippings of St. Edmund's nails, Thomas Becket's penknife, relics to stop rain, and relics to stop weeds growing in the corn.

Like more and more people at this time, this writer clearly did not believe that relics had the power to work miracles. Instead he called them *"vain superstitions."*

A new Church

The new spirit of doubt and dissatisfaction led to great changes. In 1517, Martin Luther (1483–1546) began an attack on the way in which Pope Leo X was raising money to pay for new building work on St. Peter's Church in Rome. He accused the Catholic Church of *"hopeless wickedness"* and corruption. Luther went on to develop ideas that were opposed to many basic Catholic beliefs. *"I say that no pope, no bishop, nor any other person,"* he wrote, *"may impose belief on a Christian man."*

At a time when the Bible and Church services were in Latin, Luther also wanted people to be able to understand their religion, instead of having to rely on

This is the great Protestant leader Martin Luther preaching. Luther criticized the Catholic Church of Rome and eventually broke away from it. This was a very great change.

what they were taught by monks and priests. Because of this, he translated the Old and New Testaments into German. He also believed that education was very important.

Many Protestants wanted to worship God in a very simple way. They did not want statues of saints or other ornaments in their churches. In many parts of Europe, statues like these were pulled down and destroyed.

Many people realized that Luther's teaching challenged the authority of the pope so much that it would divide the Church. Writing in Spain, one observer put it like this: *"I fear that this disagreement will be completely incurable."*

He was right. Pope Leo ordered that Luther's writings should be burned and that Luther himself should be excommunicated (cut off from the Church) if he did not withdraw his opinions. But Luther and his increasing number of supporters would not be silenced. The men and women who "protested" against the beliefs of the Catholic Church established their own Church and their own way of worshipping God. Never before had the Catholic Church been challenged by another Christian Church in western Europe.

The Protestant religion was adopted in England, Switzerland, Scandinavia, and a number of other places. Elsewhere the Protestants formed only a tiny minority. Their beliefs were feared and hated. Did you notice that Luther's teachings were described as *"poison"* by the historian quoted at the beginning of this chapter?

THE ALCHEMIST

The activities of a famous alchemist are described in this letter written in the sixteenth century:

It is rumored that this man can turn base metals into gold, and his services are much in demand. This is his recipe. He takes ten ounces of quicksilver [mercury], puts it in a fire, and mixes it with a secret liquid that he carries in a flask. It promptly turns into gold.

Turning metals into gold

Alchemists believed that it was possible to change one substance into another. Starting from this belief, they thought it might even be possible to turn base (non-precious) metals into gold, if only they could discover how to do it. Many experiments were conducted in the hope of bringing this wonderful change about. In 1565 an alchemist dedicated a book to Queen Elizabeth I of England that was about his search for the ingredient that would turn base metals into gold. She was very impressed by his ideas and asked him to make some gold for her every year!

Experiments and fairy tales

In the sixteenth century, more and more people began to be very scornful of the alchemists. The Dutch scholar Erasmus had no patience with their beliefs. Neither had the Italian painter and sculptor Leonardo da Vinci, who was also interested in science and who said that alchemists *"deceived the multitude with false miracles."* There were alchemists, like the one described in the letter at the beginning of the chapter and the man who worked for Queen Elizabeth, who tried to cheat the public, pretending that they had found a way to make gold. But there were also many people who

This woman is looking after the fire as part of an experiment. Alchemists had ideas that seem strange today, but their beliefs led them to conduct scientific experiments. This was an important new development.

These are alchemists at work. They believed that one substance could be changed into another. Some even hoped to turn base metals into gold.

were prepared to believe these claims. Our letter writer had his doubts, but in the end he was convinced. He admitted:

I am sure that this will appear mighty strange to you. It indeed sounds like a fairy tale, but you must believe me, for it is all so obvious that it cannot be doubted.

In this case the alchemist convinced everyone that his experiments worked. Only after several months did he make mistakes that showed he had been lying.

From alchemy to science

Nowadays it seems that alchemy must have been based on superstitious nonsense. Yet it interested many educated people at the time, and the alchemists did play a part in creating new scientific ways of looking at the world. They were among the first people to conduct experiments, even though they did so for very unusual reasons.

Asking questions about the world

The Renaissance spirit of curiosity affected the way in which scholars studied the world around them. They began to believe that the universe operated according to rules that they could understand through careful research, observing and recording what they saw. They thought that this knowledge would enable them to control many things. The possibilities seemed endless. *"Men can do anything if they want,"* wrote the Italian painter and architect Alberti.

This attitude marked a great change. Previously, scholars had such great respect for tradition that they had been content to accept the ideas handed down to them. The Church had influenced many of these ideas, silencing opinions that it did not approve.

But now people began to ask questions and want to find solutions for themselves. They studied newly discovered scientific texts from ancient Greece. Sometimes these writings differed from the ideas that were taught in the universities. Who was right? Questions like this also led scholars to experiment and examine evidence for themselves.

Artists were some of the first people to look at science closely. Leonardo, the critic of the alchemists, did exactly this. He studied anatomy and advised other artists to do so. *"It is indispensable to a painter,"* he wrote. Leonardo was interested in many scientific questions and carried out experiments to try to find the answers.

In the fifteenth and sixteenth centuries, people began to look at the world around them in a new way, asking questions about what they saw. This study of different plants was made as a result of careful observation.

THE WITCH

Here a sixteenth-century bishop expresses a fear that was very common at this time—the fear of witches:

The number of witches has become enormous. Within the last few years their number has marvelously increased.

Terrifying visions

The bishop was not unusual in his belief. Everyone accepted that there were supernatural forces. You can see this in the description written by a man from Spain in the 1580s:

These women were accused of being witches. Witches were believed to work with the devil. They were blamed when illness or disaster struck.

All the people saw a terrifying storm, and a large cloud. In the cloud they saw a great many evil spirits. Some were shaped as lions, others as wolves, ravens, and men.

Many people believed that strange sights such as these were signs that important events were about to take place—a battle, or the death of a prince, for example. Nearly everyone was superstitious, from kings and popes to the peasants in the countryside.

Religion and magic

It was sometimes hard to see the dividing line between religion and magic. Most people had no education and could not read the Bible or understand the Latin services of the Church. So it was easy for them to look upon Christianity itself as a form of good magic. This way of thinking influenced many people's actions. For instance, church bells were sometimes rung to ward off thunderstorms, and pieces of the consecrated Host from the Mass were placed among the crops in the belief that

they would keep caterpillars away. Above all, people looked to the Church to protect them against the devil and evil spirits.

"The land is full of witches"

Many parts of Europe were troubled by the fear of witches in the fifteenth and sixteenth centuries. In some countries, like Germany, this fear became almost a panic. *"The land is full of witches,"* wrote one worried soul.

Witches were women who were believed to receive evil powers from the devil. Records made at the trials of women accused of witchcraft tell us about the sort of problems they were held responsible for:

The witch killed many cattle, by rubbing them with ointment. She also killed the village pigs and geese by making them run over a cloth she had anointed. She brought hailstorms on the fields and made many children die.

When the crops failed, or other disasters happened, people looked for someone to blame. It was too easy for suspicion to fall on old women, poor women, or women who seemed different, like the "wise" women who made herbal remedies and acted as midwives, using skills that most people did not understand.

Witchcraft was seen as a crime and a sin. The Catholic Church was especially alarmed. Popes like Innocent VIII were determined to stamp it out. People refused to speak to women who were accused of having evil powers, or they treated them cruelly. Some of these women were brought before courts of law to be tried. Those found guilty were either hanged or burned at the stake.

Finding an explanation

To the people of the Renaissance, the belief in witches did not seem strange. There were many things they could not explain. Why did crops sometimes fail? What

Old women, poor women and those who seemed different, were accused of witchcraft in many parts of Europe. They were often tortured or killed.

Many people at this time believed that supernatural powers affected everyday life. Here is a strange picture that was painted in the Netherlands during the Renaissance. Some historians think that it was painted to illustrate the supernatural beliefs of one particular religious group.

made animals sicken and die? What caused illness? Today we would give a scientific explanation for all these things, but people in the past found answers that fit in with their religious beliefs, and they believed there were evil causes for events that harmed them.

The belief dies away

The fear of witches lasted into the seventeenth century. Then attitudes to magic, religion, and science began to change, and the fear gradually died away. If you read these words written by a man who lived at this time, can you tell that he did not take the old fears seriously?

A poor old woman comes to trial. If the judge declares himself against the old folly that the devil is interested in people's cheese, butter, and pigs, there will always be some fools who think him wrong.

THE BEGGAR

This extract comes from a law passed in England in 1530:

Throughout the realm of England, vagabonds and beggars have for a long time increased and daily do increase in great and excessive numbers.

These words were written in England, but the problem of poverty was beginning to concern people in many parts of Europe in the sixteenth century.

Here are people harvesting corn in the fields. Life on the land had always been difficult. But in the sixteenth century, conditions for some people became worse, and they began to beg for food.

The problem of poverty

Most people, particularly those who lived in the countryside, usually had just enough to get by—just enough land to grow food, just enough at harvest time, just enough money to pay their taxes. They rarely had anything more than this. But by the sixteenth century there seemed to be a large number of people who were so poor that they could not even get by. They had no work and no possessions. They wandered from place to place, begging for food or money from passersby to keep themselves alive. People tried to record the numbers involved. They believed there were at least 12,000 beggars in London and 5,000 in Paris in the sixteenth century.

Different kinds of poverty

In England, beggars were divided into two groups. The first was made up of those who were old or ill and begged because they could not work. They were known as the "deserving poor." The second group was formed by those who were able-bodied (fit and healthy) but would not work. They were named "sturdy beggars." Sturdy beggars were much feared, and some had a reputation as thieves. Such beggars were given nicknames. "Hookers" carried a long hooked pole, which they used to steal clothing through the open windows of houses. Shakespeare's play *King Lear*, which was written at this time, describes another kind of beggar, the "Bedlam Beggar," who pretended to be mad in the hope of being given charity.

Charity and punishment

The Church taught that looking after the poor and sick was a religious duty. In their wills, rich nobles and merchants often left money for the poor. The Italian artist Leonardo da Vinci remembered the poor in his will. He wanted sixty poor men to carry candles at his funeral, and left some money to pay them.

Many monasteries also gave alms (charity) to the poor. Some people set up special charities, hospitals, and schools for the poor in certain towns. But charity could not solve the problem of poverty, and people became alarmed at the growing number of beggars. Different countries had their own ways of dealing with beggars. In England during the sixteenth century various "poor" laws were passed to try to stop beggars roaming the country. They ordered beggars to go back to the place where they were born. Each parish or

Extreme poverty and unemployment became problems in many parts of Europe. This picture by a Dutch artist shows a beggar and a tumble-down house. The artists of the Renaissance recorded scenes like this in a very lifelike way.

village had to pay a new tax, called the poor rate, to provide help for the deserving poor and materials for the able-bodied poor to work with. The treatment of sturdy beggars became increasingly harsh. Those who would not work could be beaten with whips, or even branded with the letter ''V'' for vagrant (wandering beggar). The most famous of these poor laws was passed in 1601.

Begging bread in misery

Laws like these helped to discourage begging. But they did not provide solutions to the many problems that caused poverty and led people to become beggars.

While historians have suggested that a rising population and a rise in the price of food were reasons for the increased poverty in the sixteenth century, others felt that the enclosure (fencing off) of land for sheep pastures was the cause. One man who thought this wrote: *''The land is fallen into a few men's hands, whereby the rest are compelled to beg their bread in misery.''*

GLOSSARY

Apprentice   A boy or girl who was sent to learn a particular trade or craft with a qualified trader or craftsman. There were many rules setting out what the apprentice would learn.

Astrolabe   A special instrument used to study the stars.

Chivalry   Rules of behavior that knights were meant to follow. They were expected to behave with special concern for the poor, the weak, and for women. However, the rules were often broken.

Classical culture   The art and learning of the ancient Greeks and Romans.

Compass   An instrument used in navigation. It helped sailors to know where they were by showing where north and other directions are.

Divinity   The study of God and religion.

Enclosure   Most land at this time was laid out in great unfenced fields. When land was enclosed, it was fenced off into separate plots. Many enclosures were made to keep sheep in.

Fortifications   High walls and other defenses. They were built to protect places like towns or castles from attack.

Guild   An association of merchants or craftsmen. Guilds had special rules about how members should learn their trades and about how much they should charge for their work.

Humanists   Writers and scholars who were particularly interested in the learning of ancient Greece and Rome. They based their own work on it.

Interest   A fee charged when someone borrows money. The person might borrow $1,000 and have to pay back $1,100—the extra $100 is the interest.

Jousting   A special competition between knights, to test their strength and skill. Two knights charged at each other and each one tried to knock the other off the horse he was riding, using a long weapon called a lance.

Knight   The most important soldier in armies of the Middle Ages and the Renaissance. He wore armor and rode a horse.

Mangonel   A weapon used to attack towns and castles. The attacking army used it to hurl stones at the enemy's defenses, hoping to make a hole in the walls so that its soldiers could push through.

Masque   A special sort of entertainment that was very popular at royal courts. It involved dancing and acting. The people who joined in wore very elaborate costumes and masks.

Money changers   People who made a living by changing money for travelers. Travelers would come to them with the coins they used in their own country, and ask to exchange them for the coins used in another country.

Navigation   Finding a way between different places. Sailors navigated their ships by using charts and compasses and by looking at the position of the stars. These things helped them to work out where they were.

Parish   A town or village with its own church and priest or vicar.

Pavilion   A large and richly decorated tent.

Pawnbroker   A person who makes a living by lending people money and charging interest on it. The pawnbroker's customers have to leave something valuable with the pawnbroker for safekeeping, to show that they mean to repay the money they have borrowed.

Pilgrimage   A visit to pray at a shrine of a saint.

Pilot-major   A sailor who has to guide a ship into a harbor.

Proportion   The balance between the size of different parts of a building. In the Renaissance, people thought that it was very important that buildings had regular, even proportions, so that they would look attractive.

Relics   Objects that were believed to have belonged to a saint—even parts of the saint's body. Relics were thought to be especially holy, and people liked to pray close to them.

Scholar   Someone whose life is devoted to study and research.

Tilting field   The arena where tournaments were held.

Tournaments   Great competitions that were held for knights to show off their skills by jousting with each other.

Usury   Lending money to someone and charging interest on it.

Vagrant   A beggar who wanders from place to place.

FURTHER READING

Boyd, Anne. *Life in a Fifteenth Century Monastery*. Lerner, 1979.

Caselli, Giovanni. *The Renaissance and the New World*. Peter Bedrick Books, 1986.

Dwyer, Frank. *Henry VIII*. Chelsea House, 1988.

Hargrove, Jim. *Ferdinand Magellan: First Around the World*. Children's Press, 1990.

Odor, Ruth S. *Learning about Castles and Palaces*. Children's Press, 1982.

Raboff, Ernest. *Michelangelo Buonarroti*. HarperCollins Children's Books, 1988.

Richmond, Robin. *Introducing Michelangelo*. Little, Brown, 1992.

Sabin, Francene. *Renaissance*. Troll Associates, 1985.

Sendak, Cass R. *Explorers and Discovery*. Franklin Watts, 1983.

INDEX

PRINTED IN BELGIUM BY

proost
INTERNATIONAL BOOK PRODUCTION